There were a lot of other people with Clifford and his mum. They were all going to the same place. Kids with bags. Kids with gas masks. Kids with labels pinned to their clothes. Kids laughing. Kids crying. Kids holding their mothers' hands.

"Have you got your gas mask?" Clifford's mum asked.

"Yes, Mum," said Clifford.

"And your clean hanky?"

"Yes, Mum," repeated Clifford.

"And your books?"

"*Yes, Mum!*"

At the station, the children said goodbye to their parents. They were being sent away to keep them safe from the air raids.

"Write to me," Clifford's mum said with tears in her eyes.

Clifford felt empty. He knew he was going somewhere safer. But he couldn't imagine what it would be like.

All the children boarded the train. More mums and kids began to cry and everyone was waving. Clifford waved too. "I *will* write, Mum," he shouted.

The train left Liverpool. It stopped at many little stations. At each stop, names were called and some children got off. Soon only a few remained. Clifford was one of them.

Finally, the train halted at a little place called Wilton. The last children disembarked and were taken into the village hall.

There were people all around – waiting. Among them was a big man with a boy. Clifford's name was called. "Right," said the big man, "you're with me."

The man's name was Mr Ross and he was a farmer. "This is Jack," Mr Ross said. "He's my son."

Jack looked Clifford up and down. "He's a bit weedy," he said.

Clifford felt angry. He looked at Jack's dirty hands and his red face. He looked strong and healthy. Clifford's own hands were thin and white.

The three of them got into an old van. It stank of muck and pigs.

Heroes

Contents

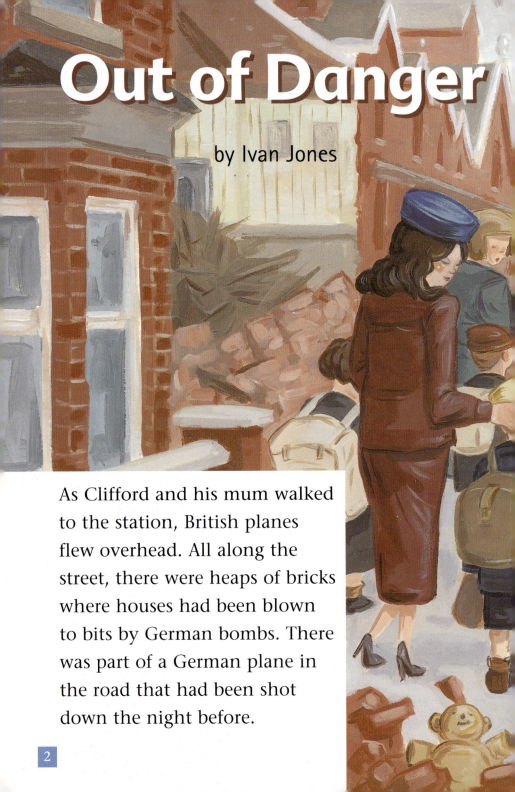

Out of Danger

by Ivan Jones

As Clifford and his mum walked to the station, British planes flew overhead. All along the street, there were heaps of bricks where houses had been blown to bits by German bombs. There was part of a German plane in the road that had been shot down the night before.

"Hey, Dad," Jack said. "Will he be any good?"

Mr Ross laughed. "I doubt it," he said.

"Don't know why we have to keep a kid," Jack said.

"Part of the war," said Mr Ross. "We all have to do things in war that we don't want to do."

Clifford felt very lonely, and rather scared.

At last they reached a muddy track that led to an ugly little house. Chickens were roaming in the garden.

"Come on, then," said Mr Ross.

They went inside the
house. There were dead
rabbits hanging from the
beams. Clifford couldn't
take his eyes off them.

"Hello," said Mrs Ross. She was a tall woman
and she wore an apron.

"Hello," Clifford said quietly.

"So what's your name?" she asked.

"Clifford."

"And how old are
you, Clifford?"

"Nine," Clifford
replied.

"Oh, same as Jack," she said. "Well, sit down, Clifford. You must be tired." And she gave him a cup of tea and some bread and butter. "You'll be able to help us around the farm," she said. "We need an extra pair of hands."

"I'll take him rabbiting, first thing," said Jack, laughing.

Mrs Ross frowned at him.

"There'll be wood to chop," Mr Ross added, "and hay to shift."

"I'll do my best," Clifford said.

"Good lad," Mrs Ross smiled.

Jack pulled a face.

Mrs Ross showed Clifford his room. It was tiny. There were blackout curtains at the window to prevent German planes from spotting the house. Clifford noticed there was no electric light, only a candle. He unpacked quickly and went back down the narrow stairs.

"Where's the toilet?" he asked.

"Down in the yard," said Jack. "There's a bucket in the little shed."

Clifford blushed and Jack laughed. Then Mr Ross came and told Jack to take Clifford out and show him round.

Jack led Clifford to a wood where they stopped by a huge tree.

"Look up there," said Jack. "That's my tree house."

Clifford could see a house high up in the branches. Jack began climbing up to it. He used a rope, and steps made out of nails knocked into the tree trunk.

When he got to the top, Jack called down to Clifford. "Come on, then."

But Clifford didn't like the look of the rope.

"Don't be a baby!" Jack yelled.

But Clifford didn't move.

"Scaredy! Baby!" shouted Jack.

That night, Clifford lay awake. He felt like crying. He wanted to go home. He got out of bed, lit a candle, and wrote his mum a letter.

Dear Mum,

I got here safely I'm with a family called Ross and I don't like them. I want to come home.

The boy is called jack and he's mean to me. There is no proper toilet. They don't even have a tap. They have to get their water from a pump in the garden. I miss Liverpool.

Mrs Ross asked me to tell you to send some money for my keep. I've given her my ration book already.

I miss you.

Lots of love,

Clifford

The next day, Jack took Clifford rabbiting.

Jack set nets over the rabbit holes. Then he sent a ferret down one of the holes to make the rabbits run out into the nets.

"Aren't you going to help me?" Jack asked.

But Clifford wanted to let the rabbits go.

"You're a real weed!" Jack said. "You can't catch rabbits or climb a tree. What *can* you do?"

"I can read and write!" said Clifford.

Jack went quiet. He couldn't read much and he could only write his name and a few words.

"Well, you're no good on a farm, that's for sure!" he shouted. "City twitty!"

Next Monday a letter came from Clifford's mum.

Dear Clifford,

Thank you for your letter, darling.

I know it must be hard for you. But keep trying, Son.

Things are bad here. German bombers have been coming over. Mrs Oliver's house was bombed and a lot of people have been killed.

A letter arrived from Dad today. He's all right, thank goodness

Are you eating your greens?

I'm sending some more money to Mrs Ross.

I'll come to see you soon.

Lots of love,

Mum

A few days later, Jack and Clifford went to the tree house again. Jack was showing off. He climbed quickly up to the top of the tree.

"I'm a bomber!" he shouted. "I'm dropping bombs on you!" And he threw twigs down at Clifford.

Suddenly, Jack's feet slipped from under him. He tried to save himself, but he couldn't. Clifford watched in horror as Jack fell through the tree, bumping down from one branch to the next. It looked as though he was going to fall to the ground.

Then he stopped. His short trousers had got caught on a branch and he was left dangling. He couldn't move.

"Jack! Jack! Are you all right?" Clifford shouted.
But Jack didn't answer.

Clifford was terrified. He wanted to run for help, but he was afraid Jack might fall even further.

So Clifford took a deep breath. Holding the rope in his hands, he began to climb the tree very slowly, not daring to look down.

At last, he reached Jack's branch. Clifford saw that he had a bad head wound.

"Jack! Jack!" Clifford shouted.

But there was no reply.

Then Clifford did the bravest thing he'd ever done. He climbed onto the branch under Jack and crept towards him. He crawled forwards slowly. The branch creaked. Clifford's heart was thumping.

At last he reached Jack. He tried to grab his jumper but it ripped. So he had to crawl even further along the branch. He lifted Jack up so that his trousers were free. Jack groaned and opened his eyes. Clifford held onto him and hauled him up to sit on the branch.

"Careful!" Clifford panted. "Hold on to me."

He pulled Jack until he was sitting with his back against the tree trunk. "I'm going to get help," Clifford said gently. Then, trembling, he climbed down and ran to fetch Mr Ross.

Soon Clifford returned with Mr Ross who ran through the wood, carrying a ladder and puffing and gasping.

"He's over there," Clifford yelled.

Mr Ross quickly climbed the ladder. When he reached Jack, he lifted him onto his shoulder. Then, very slowly, he descended the ladder and carried him home.

Jack was put to bed and the doctor was called.

"He's very lucky," the doctor said. "If he had fallen to the ground he could be dead."

"You saved Jack's life," Mr Ross said gruffly.

Mrs Ross gave Clifford a hug and began to cry.

A few days later, Jack was feeling much better. "Thanks for helping me, Clifford," he said. "You were brilliant."

Once Jack was well enough to return to school, the two boys stuck together and Clifford helped Jack with his reading.

One day, Clifford's mum arrived at the farm. "I've come to take you home, Clifford," she said. "Things are improving in Liverpool. The bombing has stopped and your school has re-opened."

Clifford was sad to be leaving.

"I'll miss the farm," he said. "And I'll miss you, Jack."

"I'll miss you as well," Jack replied.

"You are

welcome to come back and stay," said Mrs Ross. "Any time you like."

"And when the war is over," Clifford said, "You can all come to visit us in Liverpool."

And that's just what happened.

THE CHRISTMAS GI

by Dennis Hamley

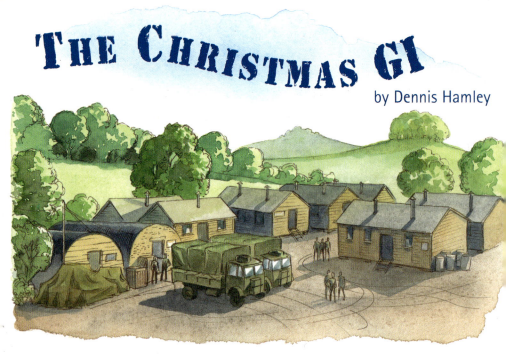

It was December 1943 and the war was four years old.

The Americans had come to Winsley, where Rose lived. Now there was an American Army camp on one side of the town and an RAF bomber base on the other. Winsley folk felt their world had been turned upside down.

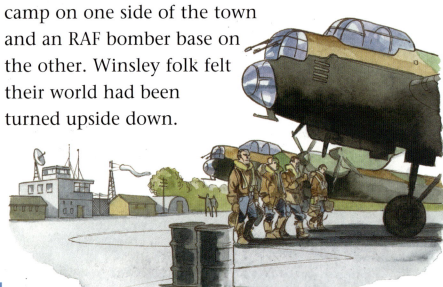

Rose was ten. Her family had arrived two years before, on a rainy day in 1941. The Air Ministry had sent her dad to look after the telephones on the RAF base. At least it was out of the way of the air raids in the city.

Rose, Mum and Dad lived in a cottage near the base. It was all right to start with. Then Auntie Vera arrived with her son, Tom, to escape the bombs in London. Suddenly the cottage seemed rather full.

Soon there was yet another member of the household. The Air Force didn't have room for all of its people to sleep  on the base. Some were sent to live with families in the town. This was called *billeting*. Into Rose's cottage came - Maisie.

Maisie was in the Women's Auxiliary Air Force – the *Waafs*. She was twenty-one and had long dark hair, which the Air Force insisted was tied up at the back. Maisie was always laughing. She and Rose hit it off straight away. She took Rose's mind off Tom, who was getting on her nerves.

Still, she shouldn't be hard on Tom. His dad, her Uncle Bill, was away in the Army, fighting in Italy. Rose knew that Auntie Vera and Tom worried that Bill might be killed. Whenever Tom saw American soldiers, or *GIs* as they called themselves, in the town, he felt angry and he would mutter.

"Why aren't they in Italy, helping my dad?"

"We mustn't ask them that," said Rose. "We must say, 'Got any gum, chum?"

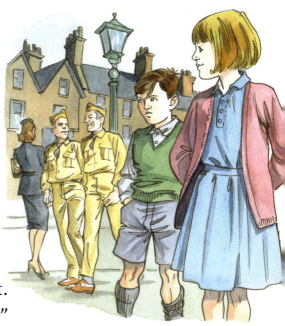

"You wouldn't dare," said Tom.

"I bet I would," said Rose, and she went up to a huge US army sergeant and said it straight out. "Got any gum, chum?"

"Sure thing, missy," said the sergeant, and produced two bars of chewing gum.

"See?" said Rose. "Easy!"

As they chewed on the gum, Tom said, "What are you getting for Christmas?"

"I don't know," said Rose. "What about you?" Tom didn't know either, and as Christmas was only two days away, Rose thought she'd better ask when they got home.

"Ask Father Christmas, not me," said Mum.

Auntie Vera and Mum were looking admiringly at Maisie who was dressed up to go out.

The children had never seen her in a frock before. She was always in her blue uniform with her hair up, not down with a flower stuck in it. Rose thought she looked beautiful.

"Don't miss the bus," said Auntie Vera.
Maisie dashed out, shouting, "See you later."
"Have a lovely time," Mum shouted.

"Where's she going?" asked Tom.
"A dance on the American base," said Rose.
"The Waafs are going in a big coach."
"What about the RAF men?" asked Tom.
"They're not invited," said Rose. "It's for Waafs and GIs."
"That's not fair," said Tom. "Anyway, what does GI stand for?"
"General Infantry," said Rose. "I thought everybody knew that."
"What does it mean?" asked Tom.
"It means a GI is a soldier who marches everywhere and carries a rifle. Like your dad."

Christmas Eve was sharp and cold. Rose didn't hear Maisie come home but at breakfast she was bright and bubbly. Her eyes sparkled with some wonderful secret.

Breakfast was the usual bubble-and-squeak made with cabbage fried up with potatoes. They munched in silence. Eating was too serious for talk.

After Mum had poured the tea, Rose asked what she was bursting to know. "Did you enjoy the dance, Maisie?"

"Gee, yes," said Maisie. "It sure was swell!"

"Yanks talk like that," said Tom. "You're not a Yank."

"Don't be rude, Tom," said Auntie Vera.

Maisie turned to Mum. "Can I bring someone round here tomorrow afternoon?" she asked.

"But tomorrow's Christmas," Tom burst out.

"I won't tell you again, Tom," said Auntie Vera.

"Of course you can, Maisie," said Mum. "Is it a he or a she?"

"Wait and see," Maisie replied.

"It's a GI," said Tom. "Will he have any gum?"

"Tom –" started Auntie Vera.

"Beats me why our own people aren't good enough for you," said Dad.

Mum looked at him furiously.

Then he stood up. "I'm off to collect the chicken from the butcher, so I can pluck it and gut it ready for your mother to cook."

Christmas Day was lovely. Rose and Tom woke at four in the morning and scrambled for the pillowcases at the bottom of their beds.

There wasn't much in either. Books for Rose, printed on scratchy grey paper, with a sign inside saying *war economy*. Tom had a book too – *How to Build Model Aeroplanes out of Odds and Ends*.

The Christmas post arrived. Mr Jenks, the postman, came in for a glass of sherry.

"I've got something for you," he said, and handed a battered brown envelope to Auntie Vera.

"It's from Bill!" she cried, tearing it open. "He doesn't say much ... But he's all right, thank God." She looked at the date. "Well, he was when he wrote this."

They had bacon and eggs for breakfast. Rose and Tom couldn't remember such a breakfast. Rose knew Mum and Vera had saved the egg and bacon rations so it could be special.

"What about presents under the tree?" Tom asked, when he had wiped the plate clean.

"Go and look," said Rose's dad.

The Christmas tree was a branch from a yew tree Dad had found in the churchyard. Rose and Mum had put it in a pot and added a few decorations which had lasted from before the war. Maisie had got coloured ribbons, which she tied on with flowing bows. There was one parcel under the tree. It was a very strange shape.

"Open it, Tom," said Dad.

Tom tore open the paper, to reveal a model battleship made of wood and painted dark grey, with turrets with tiny guns. A German flag flew from the masthead.

"I don't want a *German* ship," Tom snorted disgustedly.

"Pull the knob on the side," said Dad.

Tom did. At once, guns, turrets, funnels and the flag flew up in the air, landing higgledy-piggledy on the floor.

"You can torpedo it whenever you like," said Dad. "Then you can put it together again afterwards,"

Tom looked at it, impressed. "Gosh, thanks, Uncle George," he said. Now he felt like he could really contribute properly to the war effort!

"Is there a present for me too?" asked Rose.

"Come out into the backyard," said Mum.

Outside, Rose shouted with joy. A bicycle! She hadn't dared expect it. True, it was second-hand and a bit battered. But what did that matter? "Oh, thank you, thank you!" she cried.

The Christmas dinner was very special. The chicken with Mum's home-made stuffing was wonderful, and the vegetables from the garden went down a treat with Auntie Vera's special gravy. When they sat round the wireless to hear the King's broadcast, they were all full up.

The King's speech ended, and Dad stood up for the national anthem. Then there was a knock at the front door.

"Stay where you are till the anthem's over," Dad commanded.

Then Maisie darted off. She returned leading a tall, lean man in a light brown uniform.

"This is Dwight," she said proudly.

"Got any gum, chum?" asked Tom.

"Sure have, sonny," he said, giving Tom a whole packet of chewing gum. Dwight instantly became Tom's friend for ever.

"Gee, thanks, mister," he said. Then came the question which burned in his soul. "Why aren't you in Italy, helping my dad?"

"Don't be rude, Tom," Vera snapped. "I'm so sorry," she said to Dwight.

"That's all right, ma'am," Dwight replied. "Don't worry, Tom, we'll be helping your pop pretty soon. Only it won't be in Italy."

Dad was suddenly interested. "Will it be in France?" he asked. "Are you going to drive Hitler out?"

"We sure are," said Dwight. "You folks and us GIs together. That's what I'm here for."

There was silence. Rose had visions of her Uncle Bill and Dwight marching forward together, rifles firing.

Mum broke the silence. "Anything to eat for anyone?"

Mum and Vera made sandwiches out of the remains of the chicken. Dad brought out two bottles of light ale. Dwight could do no wrong for him now.

The evening wore on peacefully. Dwight told them of his home in Seattle, and Dad told Dwight about his job on the air base.

At last, Dwight said, "Excuse me, ma'am. I promised Maisie I'd take her out tonight, and I think the time has come."

So they left, and there was silence.

Then Dad said, "That Maisie really likes him."

Auntie Vera sighed. "They're a couple made in heaven," she said.

New Year came and still the war thundered on. But now the Allies were winning. Surely the war was on its last legs now.

Maisie and Dwight were together whenever they could be.

"Is he the one for you, Maisie?" asked Auntie Vera.

"Sure is," Maisie answered. She talked American all the time now.

In March came dreadful news. Uncle Bill was missing in action.

"It doesn't mean he's dead," Mum told the grief-stricken Vera.

"He is, I know he is," Vera sobbed. Then she wiped her eyes. "Tom mustn't know. I'll tell him his father will turn up soon."

Tom was to turn eight in May. As his birthday approached, everybody knew that the great invasion of France was coming.

On Tom's birthday, everybody put on bright expressions. Tom was delighted with his few presents. But he was beginning to think that the best present of all would never arrive.

That evening, Maisie brought Dwight round. Dwight spoke to them all. "My unit leaves tomorrow. Final training for the great day."

Dad shook Dwight's hand. "Best of luck, son," he said. "I'm proud to have met you."

After they left, everyone was quiet. The war suddenly seemed very close.

May passed into June. Nobody was happy. They were worried about Tom's dad and Dwight.

June 5th dawned.

Mr Jenks called. "I've got another letter for you," he said.

Vera tore it open with trembling fingers. She read it quickly and gave a great whoop of joy.

"Good news, Auntie Vera?" asked Rose.

Vera hugged her. Then she grabbed Tom and lifted him right off the ground. "Your father's safe!" she cried. "He's a prisoner of war. I just hope they treat him right. When the war's over he'll be coming home!"

Rose knew that however happy they now felt, they were still thinking of poor Maisie. She had gone to work that morning after another sleepless night worrying about Dwight.

Outside, a gale blew and rain beat on the windows. Nobody slept well that night.

Next morning, the BBC 8 o'clock news on the wireless told them the Allied invasion of France had started.

June 6th, 1944. D-Day, Day of Decision, had finally arrived.

Allied troops landed in Normandy. Somewhere among the thousands of soldiers was Dwight.

Slowly, British and American troops fought their way ashore. What dreadful things was Dwight going through?

41

Maisie came home. Her face was pale.

"Everything will be all right," Rose said to her. "There was good news about Uncle Bill, and there will be about Dwight as well."

"Do you think so?" said Maisie, trying to smile.

"Of course there will," said Tom. "Dwight's carrying on where my dad left off."

Then they all smiled, because they knew he was right.

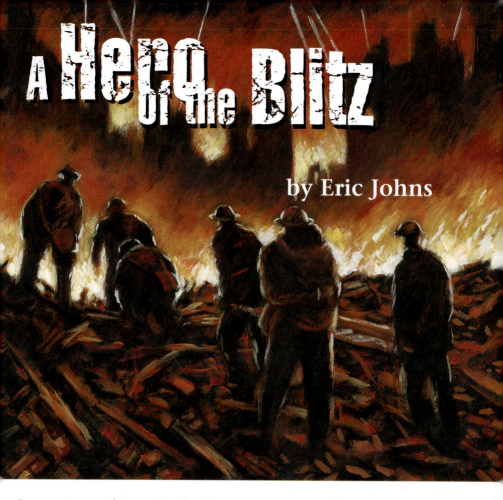

A Hero of the Blitz

by Eric Johns

I was ten when the blitz came to our house.
It was the most frightening night of my whole
life. It was also the night when I found out what
it means to be brave.

My sister, Brenda, and I had gone to bed in
the cellar. We slept down there because of the
bombing. Our bunk beds were under the cellar
stairs, because the air raid leaflet said stairs were a
good protection against bombs.

Our house was really old. There was a story that said a secret tunnel led from our cellar to the church. I didn't believe it. I had looked for the tunnel and never found it.

"Billy, I don't like it in the cellar. It's spooky," said Brenda.

She said the same thing every night. I was fed up with her saying it, so I decided to frighten her.

"There's a ghost that comes along the tunnel from the church," I told her.

"There isn't a tunnel," Brenda said. But she still cried, and Mum came and told me off.

Only Mum was at home. Our dad was away in the army. In my class at school, only two boys had dads at home. One was Tommy Colville, my best mate. His dad only had one arm because of an accident. The other boy was Philip Brown, whose dad was a coward, or so we said.

One day, Tommy and I asked Philip why his dad wasn't in the army.

"My dad's doing secret war work because he can speak German," Philip said.

"Prove it," I said.

Philip said some German words. "My dad taught me," he told us.

We stopped for a minute, not sure whether we should believe him. Then Tommy said, "His dad's a German spy."

For the rest of the day we sang, "Spy, spy, rotten spy!" every time we passed him.

That night, just after Brenda and I had gone to bed in the cellar, we heard a knock at the front door. Then Mum came down the cellar stairs.

"That was Philip's mother at the door," she said tight-lipped.

"Billy says Philip's dad's a spy," Brenda put in, trying to get me into trouble.

"So I've been hearing," Mum said. "And that's the last time anyone will hear it. Understand?"

"Yes," I mumbled. "But why isn't he in the army like everyone else?"

Mum sighed. "What's the first thing you notice about Philip's dad?"

"He breathes funny," I said.

"His chest squeaks," Brenda added, smiling up at me from the bottom bunk.

"He was in the Great War and was choked by poison gas – mustard gas," Mum told us. "He's only got half a lung that works, but he's still out helping to save people who've been bombed. How would you feel if your dad came home like that? Would you like it if people called him a spy?"

I didn't speak. I could see Mum was getting herself worked up. She was thinking about Dad ending up like Philip's dad. I'd seen her this way before, when there'd been bad war news on the wireless.

She took a deep breath. "Go to sleep," she said. "I'm going out for ten minutes, to tell Tommy's mum what you have been saying to Philip."

She pulled the blackout curtains across the gap in the wall where the cellar jutted out under the street. In front of the house there were squares of thick glass in the pavement. It was a sort of window, so we had to stop light getting out, or German planes would know where to drop their bombs.

When Mum had gone, I lay in my bunk and wondered what it was like being gassed. Gas seemed to frighten grown-ups more than bombs. We were always getting nagged about not going out without our gas masks, and each night we hung them on our bunks.

I was just falling
asleep when I heard
the sound of aeroplane
engines in the
distance. I was wide
awake at once.

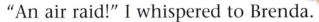

"An air raid!" I whispered to Brenda.

"There's not been a siren," she said.

But we both knew what German bombers
sounded like. Somehow they'd got through
without being spotted.

A second later, we heard the bomb coming. We
both knew what it was. We'd heard enough of
them.

First there was the whistling, like a mad dentist's
drill heading right for you. Then, at the last
moment, the whistling would always skid away,
like the drill coming out of your mouth. It would
end up in another street, with a bump that made
the cellar shake.

I was waiting for the whistling to skid away, when I suddenly thought – Mum's outside!

Then Brenda screamed, "It's not going away. It's going to hit us!"

I clutched my pillow and waited for the bump. But when it's your own house that's hit, there's not a bump but a CRACK-BANG. After that, you go deaf for a second. Then you hear a roar as your house falls down on top of you.

The last thing I saw was floorboards from the room above, splitting open like a trapdoor, and bricks starting to fall through.

I didn't see any more, because I curled up in a ball and hid under the bedclothes until the noise stopped.

I came out again when I heard Brenda coughing, and calling out, "Are you all right, Billy?"

I thought, I should be saying that, because I'm two years older, but I just said, "Have you got your torch?"

We kept torches under our pillows. I found mine and switched it on. Through the dust, I could see that the cellar looked like one of the bomb-sites where we used to play. A few inches from our bunks was a mountain of smashed up bricks and splintered wood.

"The stairs worked," I said. "They stopped anything landing on us."

But they were blocked up. We couldn't get out that way.

I knew there was usually a fire after a bomb, but I didn't say anything. I didn't want to frighten Brenda.

"We ought to see if we can get out," I said.

I could see the gap in the wall where the window was.

"I'm going to shine my torch up through the pavement glass as a signal," I told Brenda.

"I'm frightened, Billy," said Brenda.

"Let's sing 'Ten Green Bottles'," I said. "That will make us feel brave."

So we sang while I climbed over the rubble.

When I reached the window, I went to put my hand on the ledge underneath so that I could lean forward. But the ledge had vanished, and I nearly fell into a hole that had appeared there.

That was when Brenda stopped singing and said, "I can smell something."

I sniffed, and at the same time I heard a hissing sound.

"Gas," I announced. "The pipes must have broken." My voice sounded frightened to me. "Bring the gas masks!"

Brenda came tiptoeing over the rubble. She was clutching the straps of our gas masks. We quickly put them on.

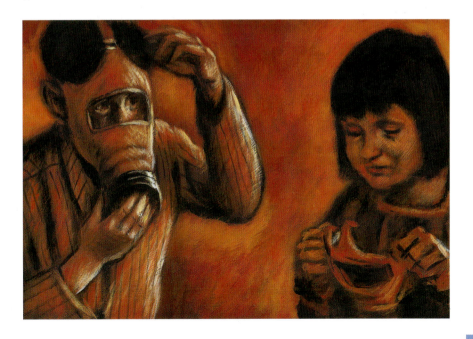

I shone my torch up at the thick glass. Through it, I could see the flicker of flames. I'd hoped the glass would be smashed, and that we could get out that way. But no such luck. We were trapped.

I flashed my torch. Three short, three long, three short – SOS. There was no reply. No one was watching.

"What's that?" Brenda's voice sounded different in a gas mask, like someone talking with their hand over their mouth.

She pointed her torch down the hole where the ledge should have been. There was a pile of rubble there, and sticking up above it was the top half of a neat brick archway.

We shone our torches through it. A tunnel led under the pavement away from the house.

I pulled the rubber of my mask off my cheek so that Brenda could hear me properly.

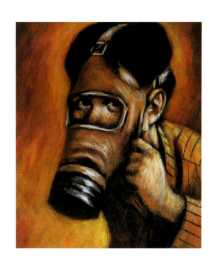

"The tunnel!" I exclaimed, feeling giggly with relief. "The story is true. There is a tunnel!"

The smell of gas was so strong, one mouthful made me feel sick. It wasn't the same as the poison gas that had got Philip's dad, but we had to get out quick in case it exploded.

We clambered over the rubble and peered along the tunnel. It was straight and dry.

Just then, we heard a hoarse voice calling from somewhere up above the cellar.

"Hello. Is anyone down there? Can you hear me?"

"It's Philip's dad," I said.

"Gas!" Philip's dad called. "You must get out – quickly!"

But we couldn't get out. There was only one way we could go, and that was along the tunnel.

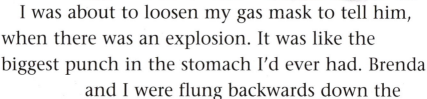

I was about to loosen my gas mask to tell him, when there was an explosion. It was like the biggest punch in the stomach I'd ever had. Brenda and I were flung backwards down the tunnel, and for a few moments we just lay there, gasping for breath.

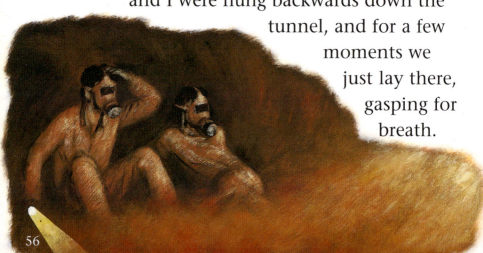

Eventually, I pushed myself onto my hands and knees. My torch was lying nearby, flickering in the darkness like the last star in the universe. When I shone it on Brenda, she was examining *her* torch. It was smashed.

Behind her I could see the tunnel entrance. It had caved in. We were now trapped in a tunnel that no one knew about.

Brenda looked over her shoulder, then calmly pointed her finger down the tunnel. I think that if she'd started yelling, I'd have panicked too. As it was, I turned round and started to walk.

As we made our way along the tunnel, I found myself repeating, "Mum, be all right. Mum, be all right," in time with our footsteps. Had she come home before the bomb? Had she been blown up? Somehow, thinking about her made it easier not to think about myself.

It was hot inside our gas masks and sweat ran into our eyes. My torch only produced a dim light, and I could hardly see where we were going.

After what seemed like hours, the ground began to slope upwards. Then the tunnel ended. There was a big, flat stone, like a tombstone, blocking our way. There was no way forward and no way back.

At that moment, I felt more lost and frightened than I'd ever done in my whole life. All I wanted to do was curl up, put my arms over my head, and make everything go away.

Then Brenda said, "What are we going to do, Billy?" I could tell from her voice that she was nearly crying.

"We're going to get out," I told her. But I didn't know how.

I took a deep breath and shone my torch all over the surface of the stone. The beam dimmed and brightened. I'd just spotted a hand-hold in the stone when the torch died for ever.

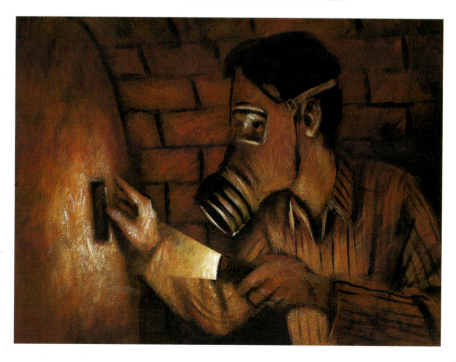

I never knew there could be such blackness.
It was like coal pressed against your eyeballs.

I felt Brenda clutch my pyjama jacket. "Don't
leave me, Billy," she whispered.

I closed my eyes so that I couldn't see the dark,
and forced my hands to search blindly over the
cold stone. After what seemed like the longest
nightmare of my life, my
fingers fitted themselves
into the hand-hold.

I pulled at the stone and
it moved. When I opened
my eyes, I saw that a
night-time dimness
had appeared.

We stepped through the gap where the stone had been.

"We're in the church!" Brenda cried.

She was right. The church was just two streets away from home.

When I let go of the stone, it swung back into place. We couldn't see exactly where we were because it was still very dark, and our gas masks made things worse. We had to feel our way round the pews until we found a door.

Outside, there were fires. People were shouting, and there were mountains of bricks which had once been houses. We held hands and ran towards home.

When we came to our street, there was a gap where our house should have been. It was like a tooth had been taken out.

"Where's Mum?" screamed Brenda.

I found Mum standing in the middle of the road, twisting a doll in her hands. Tears were running down her face.

"Mum!" I tried to say. Then I realized no one else was wearing a gas mask. I peeled it off. "Mum, you're all right!"

She turned and gazed at us. "Whatever are you doing out here?" she stammered. Then she grabbed us and we all hugged madly.

I saw a stretcher being carried away from the pile of rubble that had been our house. There was a man lying on it. I could see his face by the light of the flames. It was Philip's dad. I remembered him shouting to us before the explosion.

Suddenly, I realised that I'd done something I could never put right. I began to sob.

That was the night the blitz came to our house.

I never saw Philip again. He and his mum went away to live with his granny. I felt glad about that at the time, because I didn't know how I could have faced him. I was ashamed of myself. I'd said his dad was a spy.

After that night, I realised that you couldn't tell who was brave just by looking at them.

Philip's dad hadn't looked like much, but he'd risked the gas explosion to try to save us.

Even Brenda hadn't panicked when we were trapped underground, and she was frightened of the dark.

And me?

Well, I managed to open the stone into the church, even though every instinct in me was yelling, "Give up! You're going to die in this tunnel."

So you never can tell. One day, you might find that you can be brave too.